The
Cult
of the
Right
Hand

Doubleday

new york

london

toronto

sydney

auckland

The
Cult
of the
Right
Hand

elaine terranova

PUBLISHED BY DOUBLEDAY
a division of Bantam Doubleday Dell Publishing Group, Inc.
666 Fifth Avenue, New York, New York 10103

DOUBLEDAY and the portrayal of an anchor with a dolphin are
trademarks of Doubleday, a division of Bantam Doubleday Dell
Publishing Group, Inc.

Grateful acknowledgment is given to the following magazines, in which earlier versions of these
poems have appeared:

American Poetry Review: "The Cult of the Right Hand"; Boulevard: "Good Girl" and "A
Holy Day"; Confrontation: "Up the Block"; Hollow Spring Review: "Fire"; Kalliope:
"Dinner at the Holiday Inn"; Outerbridge: "Steven"; Painted Bride Quarterly: "A Schoolgirl
Writes to a Prisoner"; Passages North: "Pearls"; Pennsylvania Review: "Picking Strawberries";
Poetry Northwest: "Autumn Moths"; Slow Motion Magazine: "The Basement at Jordan
Marsh"; Southern Poetry Review: "The Rocking Chair" and "On Market Street"; South
Florida Poetry Review: "Shells"; Spoon River Quarterly: "1939" and "The Print Skirt";
Yarrow: "At the Grandparents'."

"Spring Rite" was first published as "Spring Assembly" in South Florida Poetry Review;
"Wedding Trip" was first published as "The First Trip" in Yarrow.

"1939" has been included in Blood to Remember: American Poets on the Holocaust,
edited by Charles Fishman (Texas Tech Press, 1991).

"Street Mural" received third prize in the 1989 Ann Stanford competition and was published in
the Southern California Anthology.

The author gratefully acknowledges fellowships in literature from the Pennsylvania Council on the
Arts and a residency at the Ucross Foundation which aided in the completion of this work.

Thanks also to Nadia Kravchenko, who typed the manuscript.

Library of Congress Cataloging-in-Publication Data
Terranova, Elaine.
        The cult of the right hand / Elaine Terranova.
        p.   cm.
        I. Title.
    PS3570.E6774C8   1991   90-43078
    811'.54—dc20   CIP

ISBN 0-385-41811-6
ISBN 0-385-41812-4 (pbk.)

BOOK DESIGN BY CAROL MALCOLM

Winner of the Walt Whitman Award for 1990

*Sponsored by the Academy of American Poets,
the Walt Whitman Award is given annually
to the winner of an open competition among American poets
who have not published a first book of poems.*

Judge for 1990: Rita Dove

For Lee

And for all my mothers —
Sadie, Sylvia, Vera, Concetta

contents

I

II

III

IV

The
Cult
of the
Right
Hand

I

*t*he rocking chair

My father has just come in from work.
I am still small, my yellow hair
only starting to darken. He pats my head
as if for luck. I see he hates
this going out each day, away from us.
His face comes back a stranger's face,
sharpened by losses, the dark beard
grown in again, defending his cheek.
I throw my arms around his neck,
wanting to reclaim him. But he turns
to my mother who sits, with all her power,
at the kitchen table. The kitchen shines

in the darkening house. Soon I come
for its protection. I bring my father's gift,
a small maple rocker. My parents' voices
clash and fall like the clatter

of forks on the luminous plates. He won't
go back again, but she is making him.
What will become of us? she says.
I'm rocking fast. The chair draws back
and sends me up into their midst.
On and on they sit with their still feet.
No one says, Watch! Take care!

The rocker moves like some mad horse.
It skims the smooth linoleum and hits
the cellar door. Open, sesame—I'm only
thinking it. The cellar opens magically.
The chair and I go hurtling down, an odd,
lopsided ride that strikes each step
into the dark. There is a cry. Overhead,
at last, the voices stop. My mother rushes
to lift me with trembling arms. Then, heavily,
my father comes. He grips the rocker,
wrenching it out from under me, and
wrestles it to pieces with his bare hands.

a holy day

At breakfast, my mother has me
turn on the gas of that cold stove
forgotten the night before. Because I am
a girl and small, this is a small sin. But
it spins me into the quickmoving world. We have

a long walk to the synagogue. I play a minute
in the arbor, in the fallen vines. Then,
as the others do, I reach and press a kiss
onto the metal case, shiny white like
the doorframe. It is a sweet word, a tickly
word to say, *mezuzah*. God lives here.

Inside, He hides behind the sliding doors.
The men sit close to Him. I am in back
among black dresses, breathing in
face powder and the smokey light. The men
begin to pray. Their backs are bent and

they are singing. Through the window I see
the twisting crabapple and its fruit that is
always small. God loves the men. He keeps
them near. God loves the old. Somehow I know
this chanting is the noise of dying. I am not

listening. I hear what I will always hear
at such a time, that stillness before the fire catches.

ire

The winter sky encircles us,
this little unit of conspirators,
this family. The backyard
ends so far from the house.
I find my four years
moving me further and further
from my mother's body.
I feel the chill that stiffens the ground
and the sleeping animals, hoping
that something of her reaches me,
at least the hot anger.

Some days the coal goes down
like black knuckles
knocking on the chute.
The fire leaps up, expecting it.

My mother stokes the furnace.
All day she straightens things,
when the wash is done, smoothing
even the obstinate cloth
with a warm iron. Each night
my father pulls his way unevenly,
lame foot after angry foot,
through the upper regions of the house.

The boys, out in the world,
practice to be men, while my mother,
in one brother's baseball jacket—
red, with "Spartans" on the back—
takes out the pliant and exhausted ash.

*U*p the block

It promised to rain.
From the door I watched
as Sheldon's mother
put out her palm to test
the sky. She raised her head
and opened and closed
her bald grey eyes like a statue's.
I came out, drawn to that other,
dark end of the block
where the dwarf lived and further on,
the adopted girl. New color
crept up the lawns to the white
rectangular houses. The branches
of the trees were long, bending down
as if to hear me. At the corner
people moved through Becker's store,
reaching for food to put

into the houses. Coming toward me

was the skinny old woman

from the next block, her face

brown and wizened like a paper bag

endlessly used, who swore

her daughter threw her down the steps

again and again. And although

I was not very good, going out

that day where I wasn't allowed,

the rain came to bless me

with all its clumsy fingers.

*p*icking strawberries

He is on a level with his children,
picking strawberries, white tennis shorts
above the black hair that coils and shines
as if with a purpose. The children
move off. The girl does cartwheels
on the grass, a movement like
the winding of a clock. The boy, with
his father's thin, slightly bowed legs
still hairless, kneels to pick two rows
away. The father gives orders in his father's
voice, smooth as glass, clear and impartial.

Like the strawberries, the children
have grown automatically, out of less.
The father has given them nothing
really he can use, his boyish smile,
a similarity of the flesh, the semen

that launched them. And now in random
offerings, just the pats and slaps,
the whole arsenal of his hands. How sweet
they are, these children, these small
beings, who haven't accumulated yet
all the continuous smells of living.

Later, his wife, the mother of
the children, notices something
disturbing about these strawberries
that have been picked. She sees them
somehow compromised, out of
the sandy ground, weeks after
the frail white blossoms
announced them. The rosy juice
that sweetens them, when they are bruised,
spills out, redder than anything. And
though she packs them away, drowsing
in boxes, it stains the boxes. Taken out
of the refrigerator, they appear
clotted with it and darkened, as if by blood.

Spring rite

It is June. We stand in line
in the schoolyard under the sun,
singing. These are
our loudest voices of the year.
The teacher waves her arms
as if to hurry us.
I am looking down at our long,
continuous shadow. I wear
my dark pink cotton dress
with its diagonal ruffle
like the sash they give

to winners of a race. These days
seedlings in pots sit
on the windowsills of our classroom.
Slowly, they are moving,
green spokes of a machine

we cannot imagine. In our
silent reading book
a boy runs off with his dog, Rags,

and a hobo. Through high weeds
they go, over country roads.
I have never seen a country road.
We are in this line
like halted marchers. For how long
must we go on singing?

*W*ild animals

"Your hair is a wild animal,"
my mother says, as if it were
luxurious and valuable,
with a life of its own and
a secret nature. She only means
it should be combed. I brush it
till it sparks. Meanwhile,
she lays out two red coats.
Like the fire in us, they shame
my father when he walks with us.

We visit mother's relative alone.
From the el, we move
down avenues and stairs
to the basement where she lives.
The dark extinguishes us.
A widow half her life, she's dressed

in it, but for the white lace collar
at her throat. Each chair we sit in
wears its shroud of lace.
Half-blind in her dim home,
she still crochets. The white twine
leads her through her life.

Like elephants, she and my mother
move carefully around each other
in the little kitchen, making
supper. They talk in low,
incomprehensible voices. Sometimes
I understand: "This is my home.
They'll take me out of it feet first."
I'm moved aside like a twig
that has gotten in the way. I sleep
surrounded by them in the one big bed,
turning all night between enormous safety
and the fear of being crushed.

*i*n the new world

There is my uncle
pulling the blue Dodge to the side
of the road, first in a family
of ox drivers to drive a car.
He is a farmer. It is
the only living he knows
how to exact from this new earth.
He is taking his corn and eggs
to market over clear, paved road.

Next to him, my aunt
in a checkered housedress
peers out through the same
wide window. Their daughter
is in back, bright
sixteen-year-old they dote on,
an American. My uncle and aunt

are thin and grey as dust.
They have poured their color
into her: red health, the grain shade
of her hair, green eyes
open to all they can contain.

What has happened
is a flat tire, some puncture
of the usual. My uncle
will jack up the ton of metal
with the strength in his back
and clever new tools.
He is an upright man, student of God
all his days. Everything waits
for him to hold it up. Behind them

someone doesn't see my uncle
pull up along the curve. Suddenly
nothing will take them any farther.
The child is dead, the farm lost.

The woman must walk in pain
the rest of her life. For years
my uncle sits more still than anyone,
hands locked between his knees.

*t*he print skirt

The zipper is the tricky part
although she knows it inside out.
Each morning she reunites
the cold metal, any time she is ready
to step out through a door. And opens
it for sleep and to change back
into herself after school. She lines up

the enormous red flowers. How bright
they are against the white piqué,
formless and somehow violent, like the blood
that spills from her body secretly
and changes it. The two back panels

join the front. She tries it on,
this skirt the shape of her. The print
wavers brokenly over her belly. Her two hands,

working only recently as a set, must judge
and smooth and unify. Then her leg presses

the thrilling pedal. The school assembly
may laugh at her when she walks in the line
of pastel shades and tiny buds and checks,
taking among them, even the boys, these
red flares. She stitches and rips. It will
never show, like teeth marks, where she tries
and tries again, like her mind learning
to worry through a thought or a desire.

II

A schoolgirl writes to a prisoner

Now when I think of you
I feel I can't move, like
I'm holding something heavy and I can't let go.

The first time you came
it was the wrong house. You wanted
someone else but I let you in. We played

checkers and we talked. You
didn't mind that I'm not pretty.
You came back, always when no one else was home

and I opened the door. By then
you were my friend. You said
what jail was like, closed off and still. The way

this house has felt to me.
Thick, cool walls, like a skeleton
on the outside of your body. You told me

that you cried. I began
to love you. I could smell
in your clothes the places you had been. Coalyards

and freight trains. When
you took them off I studied you,
black skin full of scars and marks, not empty

white like mine. For once,
you said, inside was good,
inside this house where no one could stop us, inside

my body. And then
they sent you back. I think
you wanted to go back. And could that be? Maybe

it's easier than here. The sun
goes up, comes down, there's
nothing you can do. But even here, what can

I do? Right now I feel that
something's in the house. It could
be just the wind. I hear it rattling saucers.

Or else it's like an emptying,
the air going out,
the house going flat like a flat tire. For

a long time I used to think,
and don't you think it too
when you try to sleep—at the hard thud when you

turn over—that all that
can hurt, hurts? Wouldn't it
feel good to write to me, wouldn't it steady you,

leaning like I do on this skinny pencil?

Shells

In the heat, in the high grass
their knees touched as they sat
crosslegged facing each other,
a lightness and a brittleness
in their bodies. They touched
like shells. How odd

that I should watch them say goodbye.
What did it have to do with me?

There was my own stillness
and the wasps and the tiny flies
for a long time taking stitches
in the surrounding air and

a comfort I felt, as the wind
tore through, to find the trees
miraculously regaining their balance.

pearls

One Saturday of how many,
the day is still, the sun
is pasted overhead. My friend
and I turn and turn on the lawn
waiting to be tan. We call
this game rotisserie. Beside us
are the romance and movie magazines
just let go from our hands.

We come in splotched, dizzy
with heat, not ever perfect.
Her mother is Russian and wise
and knows how to be beautiful.
"Look at yourself in the mirror,"
she says, "when you have nothing on
but pearls." Later I stare

into the mirrored door
of my mother's chiffonnier. Here
the bed linen rests like
sacramental cloth. Here my stout
mother flattens out, transcribed
to black and white. Citizenship papers,
marriage license, and stepping out
on its own, my infant footprint

on a paper from the hospital. Even
an unsuspected long-ago divorce.
(It's true the gauzy dress
that's packed away is navy and not
white.) To have gotten married twice!
That dress, so sheer, so small,
has crossed the floor a hundred times
to my room, alone, like a movie ghost.

I clasp a strand of pearls above
white flesh the shape of bathing suit,
above the startled nipples. Soon

my friend's father will be climbing
the stairs from his basement shop,

late and out of breath,
chugging up cigarette smoke
like an overworked engine. Maybe
he'll find his wife is naked
wearing pearls and call her beautiful
in whatever language they use
with one another in the dark.

Street mural

At the inside facing
of a bridge
where it rises away
from the pigeon-spattered pavement,
someone who is fifteen
has put a deer with velvet antlers.
It is looking back at him
over its shoulder.
It has the quiet, interested eyes
of his mother.

He has seen his name
sprayed across stone
like the name of a hero.
But something else
is at stake here, something
heavy with the weight

of anyone he has ever known
who has died. This is
an unlit, empty space
but he is not afraid.
He turns his back
to the unsafe street,
to dismembered, rusting cars.

Looking close, the viewer sees
there is no inside
to this deer. It is more empty
than a hunter's deer,
cleaned and trussed to a car roof.
Its hollow back
is only a reminder,
a saddle where the mind
can sit and think, "deer."
Further on, a fawn
licks at the dots
on its soft, puzzled hide.

Small tender shoots poke up
green and yellow and leaves
reach out from the sides of trees
almost anywhere, to keep
the deer alive. Some of the trees
appear to crash and fall
in the midst of these calm animals.
It does not frighten them.
All are painted
in the shiny cast-off skins
of showcard deer.
The scene is peppered
with red and blue songbirds.
In a real wood, their calls
would be a wild knocking
in the boy's heart he could wake to.

*W*edding trip

They wonder what it's like,
mountains arched before and behind them,
to live in the shadow of mountains.
The steep, perpendicular power, like some
magnetic force, holds them down,
turns them toward one another.

They sit in the square, at the last
outdoor cafe. Their backs are stiff,
not only from the cold. It's how
they are with one another. She rubs
her hands to warm them. If he
would cover them with his . . . "Where are
your gloves?" he asks.

She looks away. Two figures
in the clock tower venture out,

raising flat hammers in a simple,
parallel motion. He sees them too,
their iron capes, their patience,
their slow pursuit of one another.
For an instant the hammers pause,
undirected, as if there has been

a mechanical failure. Then they strike,
strike. At last the tinny air subsides
and the couple's view, which has shifted,
tilts back, evening the sound.
They will learn to live with cold,
with dissonance, to face the same way, to hold still.

the knot

The days come up like Quasimodo
to the tower, four flights up,
lopsided, but meaning the best.
And the tears come down,
enough to fill a cup. From where
was it borrowed, where to be
returned? In the mahogany table top
the sun is burning
its good morning.

So she gets up
and puts the breakfast on, forgetting
last night when she lay awake
until each pink violet in the flowerpot
slipped through
like a button from its hole
into nothing.

Later, the check stubs, the bills,
stained with what's
indelibly real, drop
from her fingers. The sweet
failures of every day. And she goes
to the window to look at them,
her mother did this too
at some new task, as if
to clear her sore eyes
with the light.

At six o'clock
the garlic and onions and
celery must be chopped. Blue
deepens in an elbow of kitchen sky.
She hears the first notes
of a symphony. They are
meant to shock—
the intaken breath of the violins—

he's here! Here is the boyish
smile, the bright eyes.

And her strange misunderstanding.
How they talk and how
she tries to laugh
but too much sense
like a weight
holds her mouth down.

And here is the rope that
stretches between them.
He tugs, she goes.
Then the other way. Now hilarious,
now hurt, still balancing,
they swell up in the dining room
chairs, bright and stiff
like huge balloons. Until one of them
goes mad, lets go,
flings everything—love, pain, dishes
up in the air

*i*n Greece

They saw the two chairs on the shore
then doubled back, following the line
of blazing white houses. Leaving
the car they sank a few inches into
the sand as if they belonged here,

and looked at them up close. Not
beach chairs but simple kitchen furniture,
bright with a peeling blue paint. They were
set at an angle, so that sitting in them
you couldn't look at each other. So far
apart you couldn't touch. Chairs where
fishermen mended nets or where their wives
could sit to watch the boats come in.

Maybe that day the man and woman
sat down in them and looked into the sea.
Maybe they only thought of that years

later. They didn't swim, not in such
complicated water. Far out the green
gave way to blue and then a stain
that shone like blood. Years later

they are sitting in a room. No room
is able to contain all they want from
one another. By this time strangers
have a claim on them and think of his body
or of hers as it pertains to them.

The chairs on the shore are waiting
there forever, like marble columns
holding up the past. That afternoon
they might have stayed but they could see
how poor a place it was, how no one else
was sitting by the water. And in the car
were heavy suitcases that belonged to
the people the man and woman would become.

the believer in astrology:
notes for a movie

---

1. WHEN SHE DIES

He has taken her at her word. Holds the future
shining in his palm. The knife at her throat.
Dahlias waver in the small, hinged mirror.
Sad friends, flowers. They always follow her.
They swarm before her on the bureau or
expire lightly at her wrist. The knife is thirsty,
tempered though it is in heat and quenched 500 times
to such an evenness. In all its incarnations,
never a mistake. Her breathing fogs the mirror,
wears away the landscape of her face. Dizzying, the
wound's
slow, gaudy blossoms, taking shape. The sky
is stopped, that carousel of starbound animals.

2. SUMMARY OF THE PLOT

Something has happened
at the Hotel Europa.
In Switzerland, among
the mountains. A force

moves through the corridors,
föhn, mistral, scirocco,
the exhausted breath
of an old world. It moves
from door to door, the way
that pain prowls through
the body's rooms at night.

And now the snow
is pushing in, the heavy
shoulders of the snow.
In the street dark ash
falls, a reckoning.

For years they've said,
"Poor girl. How well she does
in spite of it." They see
she gets ahead although she drags
the teeming sky along with her.
"Poor girl." And the sorrow
that's mad for her.

Not she, it's the doorknob,
the woodwork that intrude
into the room.

The Spaniard in shorts
on the bed when she opens
the door, not her husband.

3.   SHE CASTS HER HOROSCOPE

She's seated in the writing room, an alcove
of the lobby. Overhead a canary in its white cage
sings to her. She locates its small,
hiccoughing body

Her arm sweeps across the page. The sun
taps at the chart like a pointer: I go.
I see. I am. I live. I die. The straight,
dark words

She looks out the window at a view inscrutable
as the face of a stranger. A black cat runs along
the street, darting under parked cars. She's
following his broken line

Last night, the man in black jeans at the bar
and circling him, his belt of silver animals.
Her stars and planets nailed her
to the spot

Now she is fluid. Around her the wallpaper
unwinds scrolls of flowers. Maybe she has
invented them with her pen, freed them from
the notebooks she begins year after year
with the same words

She hears a vacuum cleaner suck the air into

its narrow passages. The radio says
five children have been shot in the playground
of a nearby school

She shuts the book. Anyhow, the sun is strangling
in the branches

Her past is knitting closed. In third grade,
the calf's heart that she dissected at the front
of the class is returned, whole and beating,
to the animal.

4. IN A FLASHBACK

Smoother now, the past. Where
she lived the slight rise,
the lift like the crown of a hat,
of the lawn off the street.

Bushes round as doorknobs.
Like empty spools, the trees,
when her life once wound around them.

The long shadows, the earnest miles
the sun still has to go. The way
that light and shadow work together,
joining hands around each thing.

How long she stayed, hooked,
the way a ladder and rope and
its own reflection hold a boat
to the surface of the water

while the shore climbs out,
bare, untroubled rock.

And then it was she, herself,
being looked at
from a great height.

5. IN HER OWN WORDS

We were fixed here like the trees
until snow loosened us, slipping
between us and the earth.

Tree after tree
among the many thoughts of snow.

Each week, the moon turned
to face another quarter of the sky.

I remember how the white fog
burnt, smoldering above the snow,
how it drew us to the river.

6. WATCHING HER DOUBLE

In the suburbs,
from the window that once
was hers, she sees
a small band of children drop
as if from the sky, take
the snowy hill, prowl it
like an enemy force.

And the dazzling hill shines,
brightly synthetic in the sun.

Along the low branches
the red and blue mittens fasten,
an invention, like plastic pulleys,
garish and simple. Then

the children let go, throwing
their weight in loops and arcs,
with cries, with laughter,

sliding into the sweet cold.
She watches a plump blond girl,
hair spilling from the downturned head,
who somersaults, lands with bent knees,
arms flapping out
and leaving in the snow
the outline of an angel.

She is thinking of
another little girl
as clearly blond, fairhaired,
until her luck changed.

*T*exas Department of Corrections

—*from photos by Danny Lyon*

---

1.   CHRYSALIS

Almost transparent, their thin bodies
in the white prison pajamas,
faces dark under flapping hats.
The long, delicate wings at rest,
spread behind them. These are only
sacks of cotton, filling as they pick.

2.   IMAGO

With day they wake
to better fields, richer growth,
shaking off
the soothing crust of insect sleep,
raw and new under another sun.

Nothing can hurry them,
the hours paced in unending rows,
staring down into the moist earth,
into their entrapment.
Only suddenly the shutter
is tripped, metal blades falling
like a small, harmless guillotine.

3. PRINT

At the top, a mounted guard
gives orders in slow, explicit
human speech. Light strikes,
producing the latent, still reversible
image. The moment scatters on the film,
a flickering incandescent white,
the black defense of earth
and the men's impenetrable bodies.

Some miles south windswept palms
are stopped like dark stars along the road.

*t*he week before the suicide

I don't remember his name now
or what we were celebrating.
I know his pregnant wife was there.
It was late afternoon
and everyone kept looking out
at the ragged flakes, waiting for dark.

I watched him pace, hugging the walls.
He'd hit the little knots of people,
splitting us apart, nudging us
into corners. Sometimes he'd lurch
and grip a chair and shout our own words
back at us. Each time he passed

I was afraid he'd pivot
and come back to me. He grew pale.
I could see it wasn't water,

that it was straight vodka
he was sending down. He was sweating
and he smelled. I hated him.

I think we all hated him.
The afternoon went on, the talk,
the watching him. I remember
what the room felt like, the forced-air
heat and the sting of the light.

1939

A woman takes a small girl's hand.
The leaves pull away and fall,
separate, stiff with color.
Out of the smokey, distant forest
the train brings its load of passengers,
the passengers, their burdens.
A horse nuzzles the fence of every field,
at peace within its boundaries.
There is the woman's beautiful fair hair,
a certainty that's braided into it.

Before them lies the station house,
its civil wood. At the crossing
the station master's wife aligns the bars
of any misdirected night.
A girl is walking by her mother's side.
She knows from fairy tales

the shape that evil takes—
stretched in shadow, giants, witches,
wolves—the weight of poisoned fruit,
the irrevocable claim of fire.

The hill twists and flattens.
The little girl looks at the funny hooks
of weeds, like fingers pointing down,
down. She hears the snap of branches
underfoot, the whistling stalks
that pull the air into
their tubular, dry bodies. Sometimes
in the wind the trees reach up
on tip-toe to the sky like tall, lost girls.

These are easy days. Heaven
comes to meet the earth
in such a bountiful accord. The sun
so neat it pulls the water taut
until the river shines. The two walk on
into the clouds, an ample white,
into a sky that has already forgotten them.

III

the cult of the right hand

—Ijo sculpture: Hand Cult Figure, rider of a monstrous beast (the soul). His right hand is thought to be the source of his aggressiveness and skill.

1. THE UPPER HAND

Each of us mounts his own soul,
a creature held up by impulse,
by avowal, by fantasies
of war: the spirits of ancestors,
mutilated veterans, horrific diseases.

We rejoice in the quick horn,
the muscles shining beneath the skin.
When his fangs lock, a door is shut
on our most damaging secrets.
Our enemies see in his dust
the sky rearing up in terrible punishment.

Because of his long legs
we make him carry us.
He'd rather graze the quiet fields
alone, moving slowly over grass.
In our right hands are reins,
in our left, the curved air of fear.

2. ENSURING THE WELFARE
OF THE SPIRIT

After long drought
the herd stampedes,
excited by the rain.

A man loses his cattle,
goes mad, wanders naked
through the bush.

No one can go on like that,
a darkness
always weighing one side down—

forgetting spring,
the uproar of stars
in the northern sky.

The rest of us make peace.
The table is set, the grass mowed,
the teapot whistles to warn us.

Our voices climb higher,
stronger, in the steps
of song. The cup and the fan
are sacred in the temple of our grasp.

3. RITUAL METHOD

Not to let go.
To take flowered cloth
and wring from it a beauty.
To heat the quiet carcass
until it sputters and darkens.
To peel, to strip the toughness
from anything with the heart to grow.

To soothe the young
of any species,
picking discomfort from them
with light fingers.
To see that the night is full,
for peace of mind, to cover it.
To treat misfortune
with the charms of our strange beliefs.
To lock doors
and to shore up the earth
in backyards and gardens.
To keep in every closet,
every cupboard
something hidden of ourselves.

4.   HAND CULT FIGURE

A sky in layers,
striped like an awning,
stretches over the Blue Moon Diner.
The sullen uniform approaches

(oh the mysterious silence
a waitress leaves
to come to you).

You walk in
with last money, last chances.
Then the booth
lends you a quiet dignity.
Coffee fires you with confidence.
You feel a surge of energy
as the people behind
rise, pushing away food and talk.

You stare across
at the knees of stained grey trousers,
the counter that slides toward
rustling curtains. A beam of light
through the blinds
threads the dozen or so diners.
Bright food, light.
And your own right hand

moves toward a fork,

lifts it to gather

the lemon meringue pie.

5. PASSING ON

Death is in the viewing room,

shriveling the edges of the flowers.

Gracefully it clasps the woman's waist.

It has come in a car like anyone else,

pale and in sunglasses.

Cool air swirls past

as if there were dancing.

The outer room is spotlessly clean.

When we move toward it

dark pursues us, an indoor dark,

the kind that rests in the clothes

hiding our bodies.

I scratch my arm. My fingernails

are hard and smooth, a simple reassurance

like a good thought. We are seated
on green velvet couches. Everyone smiles
and talks. The flowers next door
overflow, crowding through the doorway
close to us. Their breath is cool,
unlike ours.

This family, these faces
with her face pressed on them, like coins.
I watch them in the mirror.
Like fountains they are playing
one by one, after each green interval.

IV

*a*utumn moths

They are saying,
I have left off my hood of self-
annulment. I wish to be seen,
to see.

Our world appears to them
through the peculiar clearness
of a new season.

Legs hooked
to the window glass,
wings roof the vulnerable

body. They are
drawn to us in our lives
as we, who want to know more,
are drawn inward,

and balance by wingbeat
and pirouette
at the thin edge
of an earth

that will turn
to crush them. We
put out the light.
There is no comfort left

to them, to us—

for darkness is what
we cannot know with our hands,
not even with
the brilliant inconsistency
of fingers.

On Market Street

in front of the department store,
in the full surprise of day,
a young girl is lying
on a white sheeted hospital bed.

At first there is only
the fact of her, an impediment
to be gotten around
like a statue or accident.

But I'm stopped by the arms that end
in dull blades, the stiffness
of the form under the sheet.

Dust and sun drift down to her.
I watch her eyes fill up with light.
Then, as if she's beckoned them,
heavy footed pigeons come.

How calm she is, like a painted saint,
like a miracle she is used to.
Someone throws money in the cardboard box
a woman holds. A small boy, too,

is hovering nearby. She
is theirs. They are glad for her.
Anyone would be, seeing their hopes,
though they twist, come to some use.

They bear her along
as if all the souls in the world
corresponded in number to the stars,
each in its own vehicle.

Steven

Now when I see you,
your face so thin
that was full and smooth
when we were children—
a collapse of expectation maybe—
and the greying mustache
and great height

I remember years ago
when we played board games
in Evan's dining room,
he in his wheelchair
and I, a girl, seated
in the inescapable stillness
at the center of this.
The steel pieces moved for us,
the scotty, the shoe, the tiny

perfect iron. I remember
the hours of rehearsed journeys,
the waits and starts,
the small excitements like switches
that ignited us,
as we came to one another
out of the catacombs
of separate lives, out of

our catty-cornered houses
and I wonder how you withdrew
from that heroic, other
childhood. What took
your eye off the ball
that would surely fly
into your hand or unfastened you
from the churning skates,
the bike: How you quieted

yourself enough to play
with us. Maybe there was

something even then
of the kind patience that
in time lengthened you,
of the gentle father
who came for you. We
looked up to see the day end
in the blue stubble on his face,
not sure how long
he had stood watching us.

*t*he guest room

At night it's cold. When I wake up
half through with sleep, I'm sure
my feet have been peeled back to bone.
I rub until the blood comes into them
and wrap them in the blanket. There is
a heating duct somewhere invisible
behind the furniture. Even so, the room
seems disconnected, on its own. Especially
when snow, as if drawn to the light, swirls up
and clings, each independent flake, and then
the glass becomes another wall. Close
to the window are the blow dart, machete
and other weapons of South American headhunters.
They were brought back by the dead grandparents.
Then a picture of these grandparents
holding an infant, their arms crossed
like branches. An aunt's pastel

of the younger child, her funny, wise face,
one baby tooth just gone, hangs opposite.
In a vase on a maple table sit the pink
silk tearoses that were brought to a hospital,
still blooming, still ineffectual. Then a shelf
and books that someone's read. Last summer's
clothes are in the closet, and on the door
a cuckoo clock is strapped in its white,
silent lattice. At the bedside, between a lamp
and a piece of driftwood, the family
looks out of an antique photo, posed
in old costumes, turning away.

In the morning the goodhearted dog
is in the hall. He barks
and nudges the door open. When he sees
it's only me, he licks my hand and
goes away. Today, as on every other day,
the sun draws a little more color
from the fading blue curtains. My head
still on the pillow, I spot an old dollhouse

in the corner and stare into
its gutted rooms. I get up
and make the bed. I know by night
the sheets will seem a little mussed,
the eager fog will collect
like a breath at the window.

At the grandparents'

The baby squirms in her arms.
Again, she can almost feel him grow.

The first spring sun
stares down at them. At last
the days are even with the nights.

From the hard earth
of his garden, the grandfather rises.
This is as close as he can come.
She holds the baby up to him
as if it could warm him.

All around, green
starts up from nothing.
She looks off to the hills,
distant as they were in her childhood.

The grass slides forward
and approaches them; straight-kneed,
the tulips reach up
as if to be remembered.

Vines grow around inside and out,
tightening the little house. Everything here
the grandmother has knotted together
with bright colors.

The baby's father
moves among them, free;
all the others
are tied to one another.

When they leave
the old man bends again,
in the sun's cold aftermath,
not sure what has taken hold.

good girl

Their lives are dim and surround them uselessly,
loose fitting now like the garments
they have on, that are stiff with a kind of despair
and lock the flesh. In the end
they cannot walk. One sits. The son
and daughter try to lift her,
without conviction. Because there is no will
to rise, they let her sink again
before the fragile bones collapse
like an abandoned nest. Food comes
and the son has her open her mouth and each time
says, "There's a good girl." She tells him,
"Careful! Don't fall out of the wagon. Careful,
no one gives you ice for free."
She is striking one index finger
with the other, as if trying to start a fire.
Then she finds herself here, with them,

bewildered, begging them. The nurse comes

to hush the TV, leading

its own inconsequential life

beside them. Dark too arrives, a tide

that has crept up on a shore,

that no one is aware of. They are

underwater, under the sea

that boils everything to such an evenness.

dinner at the Holiday Inn

Not much with me, a jacket and my book.
I'm shown the window table, the exhausted sky,
someone with perfect posture arranged at the piano.
She sways. The music follows her. It cannot help
itself. I watch her flowered smock, her hidden face
tilt back and forth. She isn't good

but blond and full of pep, needed here and good
enough. I go off somewhere in the book,
as real a place as being here. A smile plays on my face
for no one. The fat notes spring into the sky
like miracle plants. Clearly, this distance is no help—
the life I've left matched theme for theme on the piano.

Hammered shut, the dark wood cabinet of the piano
may be the coffin of mismanaged deeds, of good
ideas. Or else the woman is a midwife and I help

pull myself through by listening. In front of me, the book
is closed. I read the mystifying sky
and turn and turn, not sure of what to face.

To help, I make myself a map. The faces
at the tables, the window, the piano,
and tucked into the trees, these few rags of a sky.
Then someone brings me bread. I bite into the good
hard crust. Nearby, like me, a woman with a book
is raising it to ward off blows, to rest her eyes, to help

conceal herself. And further on, an older couple, help-
mates, confidants. For many years they have been face
to face. Like reading from a book,
their rehearsed speech. I hear them over the piano.
They catalog how long each cancer takes, then have a good
    good
laugh over that, a laugh directed at the sky.

The last hills fold into the dark that fills the sky.
I watch as with a sense of purpose now the help
light candles at the tables. So little good

the small flames do, except to halo every face

and each becomes a separate solemn icon. The hands on
   the piano

smooth over it an old song, a page out of a book.

The sky has been closed utterly, a finished book.

In the window, like a ghost in a jar, is my own face.

The busboys leave their busy lives and with the kitchen
   help,

come out for air, come out for good, come out to the
   piano.

*M*issing person

Flossing her teeth, she moves
unconsciously so that her feet
at last are in the position of his
before the mirror, orthopedic shoes
pointing in different directions

as if this were a dance step
or the start of a dive, waiting for
the same inspiration that sent him off.
She enters the bedroom. The white linen
stretches endlessly before her.

Only she can say how much she's learned
from him, to glide when she swims,
to push off with longer strokes. To hold
a knife so it peels away, not turning
inward toward her chest. To find outside,

in him, a point of reference and stop
this circling back into herself. And she looks
at the phone in its hard black nest.
The cord is slack. He will never
complete the circuit. He would have to say,

"It's me," in an uneven voice, as if
he weren't sure. But she knows he would like
even now to keep her on the line
forever, never saying anything.

*t*he farm in the city

—*Farm Persevere, originally the residence
of the painter Charles Wilson Peale, 1741–1827*

G. and I follow
the routine of the sun
on its essential stops
along the edges of the yard,
out from the great
disfiguring shade of the house.

I feel I'm being kidnapped
like the watchdogs, street dogs really,
tied and roughly possessed. When it rains
he brings me in. Our soaked clothes
cool the room and give back
the scent of the flowers. He doesn't
try to kiss me. He's spent
these seven years alone, a generation,

writing. Dust cancels all his things
except the ironing board, out always,
protected with new pages.

He writes about the farm,
how the painter who built it
filled it with children
and inventions. My friend has lived
the last 200 years drawn into
the arms of happy ghosts. Each day
he looks through the window
at the vast garden and the wire fence.

Each year the neighborhood
creeps closer, dims with more
rows of buildings. Once a cow
of his broke out, bewitched,
and had to be subdued and brought back
like a convict by the police. And
sometimes now on summer nights
prowlers reach the end of concrete
and go on. The fence has tightened

around this witnessing. His book
is nearly done. I brush against
the bushes as I leave, wisteria,
those flowers that drop into the palm
like rain when you shake them, when you
even interfere with them. I find
at my feet blue petals like
a shattered longing.

*t*he basement at Jordan Marsh

The bakery is in a corner of the basement
opposite the women's room. Ahead of me
is a tiny old woman in a paisley scarf
who takes two little shuffling steps
with one foot and then a long one
with the other to catch up. Meanwhile

at the counter, a young woman is handing out
Styrofoam cups and reaching for fresh muffins.
At last, she's up to me. Hands full,
I watch the little shuffling woman move toward
the one remaining chair and settle into it
her body that age has made awkward and beautiful

like a harp. I stand at a waist-high spool-shaped
table, not old or young, and feel myself
unraveling from myself like a string ball

it has taken a lifetime to save. The muffin
is juicy with blueberries, sweet.
Above me is the heavy lid of the basement
ceiling. Long ago I put up my hands

and my mother or a saleswoman pulled over
my head for the first time this feeling
of tightness in my chest, this fear of dark.

Second marriage

She overhears the guests
who are wondering,
Where are we? Is this
the house? They seem
reassured by the lawns.

She lets them in.
There is a movement
up and down the stairs,
a sprawl throughout
the couple's life.

They eat until no food
is left. Empty beer bottles
tilt on the sill while
the singer's shrill voice
on the loop of tape
startles everyone over

and over again. Sometime
the guests will have
to leave, so they plant
remarks deep in
the furniture, even
outside, behind the shrubs

and trees. At last
the car doors close
like a summing up.
In the darkened house,
he is bending himself
to her, shielding her

from what is past,
from what is still
to come. And she,
with her whitening hair,
and plump, still receptive
body, reaches up past

herself to him. The window
fills with light, with
the bright shock of forsythia.
Her daughter is home. She thinks,
We are a statue now. This is

a permanent embrace. This way
she can withstand
the younger woman's
hardened gaze. She thinks,
In my vagina, I am always beautiful.

*t*he wild parakeets

In the evening she comes out
to the garden's ruthless growth.
Against her shears agave raise
invincible swords. She is overwhelmed

by the cannibal blossoms of bougainvillaea.
The water is pushing with all its weight
against the seawall. In a few hours
she will witness again what seems

the impossible effort of sunrise.
Nothing has noticed her, a widow, frail,
alone. Frogs in the grass are singing
to themselves. Not even the roaches scatter.

She works until her fingers ache, until,
clear of weeds, the jacaranda has been lifted up.

Then it may be a bird she hears or the iron
chirp of the empty swing. She tries to stand.

Out of the long-neglected lime tree,
wild parakeets swoop down at her
with their scalding voices. What is
this impulse, fierce and green? She's sure

the sun is at the heart of it. They
have escaped from someone's care into the heat
and light of Florida. Now free, they mate
and bear new young. Oh, shut them up,

banish them. Like the voices on the radio
that sing under her sleep all night.
But she'd take music, even music,
over this jangling dialogue.

about the author

Elaine Terranova has been an editor and a teacher
of English and creative writing, as well as an Artist in Education
in Pennsylvania schools. She teaches writing
at Community College of Philadelphia.
The Cult of the Right Hand is her first book.